Bend, Stretch, and Leap

Story by Julie Haydon
Illustrations by Meredith Thomas

South Pointe Scholars

There were lots of things
that Tommy liked to do.
He liked to read,
and watch his favorite TV shows.
He liked to play basketball
with his friends.
And Tommy liked to do ballet.

Every Saturday morning,
Tommy walked to the ballet school
with his sister, Jessica, and his mom.

The ballet teacher always stood
at the front of the class
so all the children could see her.

When the music started,
everyone would bend
and stretch and leap.

Tommy loved ballet.

One Saturday morning,
after ballet class,
Tommy walked to the store
with Jessica and Mom.
He met Jackson and Robert
from school.
They had been playing football.

Jackson laughed at Tommy.
"Have you been doing ballet again?"
he asked.

"Tommy likes ballet," said Robert.

"Ballet is for girls," said Jackson.
"Football and basketball are for boys."

“But boys can do ballet, too!” said Tommy.
“I like football and basketball **and** ballet.”

All that week, Tommy thought about what Jackson had said.
The next Saturday,
Tommy decided that he didn't want to go to ballet class.

"Are you feeling sick?" asked Mom.

"No," said Tommy.
"I just don't want to go."

So Tommy stayed home with Grandma while Jessica and Mom went to the ballet school.

But Tommy felt sad.
He missed doing ballet.
He wished he was bending
and stretching and leaping
to the music.

When Tommy arrived at school
on Monday,
Robert and Jackson rushed up to him.

"We are going to have a visitor today,"
said Robert.
"He's going to meet us in the hall."

As the children walked
into the school hall,
they saw their visitor waiting for them.

"It's Greg Stanley!" said Jackson.

"The basketball player!" said Robert.
"He's the greatest!"

"Hello, boys and girls,"
said Greg Stanley.
"I'm here to talk to you
about keeping fit.
Playing sports is a good way
to keep fit.
Let's do some quick warm-up exercises,
and then we'll play a game
of basketball."

Everyone in the class
had a turn at playing basketball.
But no one was more fit than Tommy.
He could run faster than anyone else,
and jump higher to make a basket.

After Tommy made his fourth basket,
Greg Stanley said to him,
"You are a very good basketball player!
I can see you are very fit."

"Tommy does ballet!" said Jackson.
"What do you think
of a boy doing ballet?"

Greg Stanley smiled.
"I think it's a great idea," he said.
"I learned ballet when I was a boy.
It's one of the best ways to keep fit.
And it's good for your balance, too.
What do you like best
about ballet, Tommy?"

"I like to bend and stretch and leap,"
said Tommy happily.
"Ballet is fun!"